THE RIGHTS OF MAN

THE RIGHTS OF MAN

AND NATURAL LAW

BY

JACQUES MARITAIN

LONDON
GEOFFREY BLES

TO

JOHN U. NEF

First published October 1944.
Reprinted June 1945.
Reprinted June 1958.

PRINTED IN GREAT BRITAIN BY
ROBERT MACLEHOSE AND CO. LTD
THE UNIVERSITY PRESS
GLASGOW

A SOCIETY OF HUMAN PERSONS

THIS little book is an essay in political philosophy. Given a war wherein the destiny of civilization is at stake, and given a peace which also will have to be won after the war is won, it is very important that we have a proper and firmly established political philosophy. What I propose is intended to induce those who read these pages to clarify their ideas upon a fundamental question of political philosophy—the question of the relationship between the person and society, and the rights of the human person.

THE HUMAN PERSON

I shall not here discuss many philosophical problems presupposed by my subject, notably the problem of those two metaphysical aspects: *individuality* and *personality*, which are distinct in each one of us and which create in us two attractions in conflict with one another.[1] It is essential, however, to throw light on the very notion of the person, in order to characterize briefly the relationship between the human person and society.

In each of us there dwells a mystery, and that mystery is the human personality. We know that an essential characteristic of any civilization worthy of the name is respect and feeling for the dignity of the human person. We know that in defence of the rights of the human person, just as in defence of liberty, we must be ready to give our lives. What worth deserving of such sacrifice is then contained in man's personality? What precisely do we mean when we speak of the human person?

Whenever we say that a man is a person, we mean that he is more than a mere parcel of matter, more than an individual element in nature, such as is an atom, a blade of grass, a fly or an elephant. Where is the liberty, where is the dignity, where

[1] *Cf.* my book *Freedom in the Modern World* and the chapter on 'The Human Person and Society' in *Scholasticism and Politics.*

5

are the rights of an individual piece of matter? There would be no sense in a fly or an elephant giving its life for the liberty, dignity, or rights of the fly or the elephant. Man is an animal and an individual, but unlike other animals or individuals. Man is an individual who holds himself in hand by his intelligence and his will. He exists not merely physically; there is in him a richer and nobler existence; he has spiritual superexistence through knowledge and through love. He is thus in some fashion a whole, not merely a part; he is a universe unto himself, a microcosm in which the whole great universe can be encompassed through knowledge; and through love he can give himself freely to beings who are, as it were, other selves to him. For this relationship no equivalent is to be found in the physical world. All this means, in philosophical terms, that in the flesh and bones of man there lives a soul which is a spirit and which has a greater value than the whole physical universe. However dependent it may be on the slightest accidents of matter, the human person exists by virtue of the existence of its soul, which dominates time and death. It is the spirit which is the root of personality.

The notion of personality thus involves that of totality and independence; no matter how poor and crushed a person may be, as such he is a whole, and as a person, subsists in an independent manner. To say that a man is a person is to say that in the depth of his being he is more a whole than a part and more independent than servile. It is to this mystery of our nature that religious thought points when it says that the human person is the image of God. The worth of the person, his liberty, his rights, arise from the order of naturally sacred things, which bear upon them the imprint of the Father of Being, and which have in Him the goal of their movement. A person possesses absolute dignity because he is in direct relationship with the absolute, in which alone he can find his complete fulfilment. His spiritual fatherland consists of the entire order of things which have absolute value, and which reflect, in some way, an Absolute superior to the world and which draw our life towards this Absolute.

I am not forgetting that strangers to Christian philosophy can have a profound and authentic feeling for the human person and his dignity, and even at times show by their behaviour

6

a practical respect for that dignity which few can equal. But the description of the person here outlined is, I believe, the only one which, without their being themselves aware of it, provides a complete rational justification for their practical convictions. Moreover, this description does not belong exclusively to Christian philosophy (although Christian philosophy carries it to a higher point of accomplishment). This description is common to all philosophies which in one fashion or another recognize the existence of an Absolute superior to the entire order of the universe, and the supra-temporal value of the human soul.

THE PERSON AND SOCIETY

The person is a whole, but it is not a closed whole, it is an *open* whole. It is not a little god without doors or windows, like Leibnitz's monad, or an idol which sees not, hears not, speaks not. It tends by its very nature to social life and to communion.

This is true not only because of the needs and the indigence of human nature, by reason of which each one of us has need of others for his material, intellectual and moral life, but also because of the radical generosity inscribed within the very being of the person, because of that openness to the communications of intelligence and love which is the nature of the spirit, and which demands an entrance into relationship with other persons. To state it rigorously, the person cannot be alone. It wants to tell what it knows, and it wants to tell what it is—to whom, if not to other people? We can say with Jean-Jacques Rousseau that the breath of man is deadly to man; we can say with Seneca: 'Every time that I have been among men I have returned a diminished man.' All that is true—and yet by a fundamental paradox we cannot be men and become men without going among men; we cannot make life and activity burgeon within us without breathing in common with our fellow-men.

Thus society is born, as something required by nature, and (because this nature is *human* nature) as something accomplished through a work of reason and will, and freely consented to. Man is a political animal, which means that the human person craves political life, communal life, not only

7

with regard to the family community, but with regard to the civil community. And the commonwealth, in so far as it deserves the name, is a society of human persons.

This means that it is a whole made up of wholes—since the human person as such is a whole. And it is a whole composed of liberties, since the person as such implies mastery of self or independence (I do not say absolute independence, which is proper to God). Society is a whole whose parts are themselves wholes, and it is an organism composed of liberties, not just of vegetative cells. It has its own good and its own work which are distinct from the good and the work of the individuals which constitute it. But this good and this work are and must be essentially *human*, and consequently become perverted if they do not contribute to the development and improvement of human persons.

THE COMMON GOOD

It is important that we state these ideas with as much clarity as possible.

Let us not say that the aim of society is the individual good or the mere aggregate of the individual goods of each of the persons who constitute it. Such a formula would dissolve society as such for the benefit of its parts, and would lead to an 'anarchy of atoms.' It would amount either to a frankly anarchic conception or to the old disguised anarchic conception of bourgeois materialism, according to which the entire duty of society consists in seeing that the freedom of each one be respected, thereby enabling the strong freely to oppress the weak.

The aim of society is its own *common good*, the good of the social body. But if we fail to grasp the fact that this good of the social body is a common good of *human persons*, as the social body itself is a whole made up of human persons, this formula would lead in its turn to other errors, of a collectivist type—or to a type of state despotism. The common good of society is neither a mere collection of private goods, nor the good proper to a whole, which (as in the case of the species with regard to its individual members, or the hive with regard to the bees) draws the parts to itself alone, and sacrifices these parts to itself. It is the good human life of the multitude, of a multitude of persons, the good life of totalities at once carnal and spiritual, and principally spiritual, although they more often happen to live by the flesh than by the spirit. The common good of society is their communion in the good life; it is therefore common *to the whole and to the parts*, to the parts, which are in themselves wholes, since the very notion of *person* means totality; it is common to the whole and to the parts, over which it flows back and which must all benefit from it. Under pain of being itself denatured, it implies and demands the recognition of the fundamental rights of the person (and the rights of the family, in which persons are enmeshed in a more primitive way of communal living than in political society). It involves, as its *chief* value, the highest possible attainment (that is, the highest compatible with the good of the whole) of persons to their lives as persons, and to their freedom of expansion or autonomy—and to the gifts of goodness which in their turn flow from it.

Thus we perceive a first essential characteristic of the common good: it implies a *redistribution*, it must be redistributed among the persons, and it must aid their development.

A second characteristic relates to *authority* in society. The common good is the foundation of authority; for indeed leading a community of human persons towards their common good, towards the good of the whole as such, requires that certain individuals[1] be charged with this guidance, and that the directions which they determine, the decisions which they make to this end, be followed or obeyed by the other members of the community. Such an authority, aimed at the good of the whole, applies to free men, in utter contrast to the dominion wielded by a master over human beings for the particular good of this master himself.

A third characteristic has to do with the *intrinsic morality* of the common good, which is not merely a set of advantages and conveniences, but essentially integrity of life, the good and righteous human life of the multitude. Justice and moral righteousness are thus essential to the common good. That is why the common good requires the development of the

[1] In certain cases authority may be exercised directly by the people themselves, but in such instances we are dealing with very small communities leading a very simple life, or with particular decisions to be made by 'referendum.'

9

virtues in the mass of citizens, and that is why every unjust and immoral political act is in itself harmful to the common good and politically bad. Thereby we see what is the root-error of Machiavellianism. We also see how, because of the very fact that the common good is the basis of authority, authority, when it is unjust, betrays its own political essence. An unjust law is not a law.

TOTALITARIANISM AND PERSONALISM

From the very fact that society is a whole made up of human persons, it is apparent that the mutual relationship between the individual and society is complex and difficult to perceive and to describe in its complete truth. The whole as such is greater than its parts. This is a principle which Aristotle emphasized and which every more or less anarchic political philosophy chooses to disregard. But the human person is something more than a part with respect to society. Here is another principle which Christianity has brought to light and which every absolutist or totalitarian political philosophy relegates to darkness.

Let us understand the question. A person as such is a whole, open and generous. Indeed if human society were a society of *pure persons*, the good of society and the good of each person would be but one and the same. Yet man is very far from being a pure person; the human person is a poor, material individual, an animal born more poverty-stricken than all other animals. Even though the person, as such, is an independent whole, and that which is noblest in all nature, the human person is at the lowest level of personality, stripped and succourless; a person destitute and full of needs. Because of these deep lacks and in accordance with all the complements of being which spring from society and without which the person would remain, as it were, in a state of latent life, it happens that when a person enters into the society of his fellows, he becomes a *part* of a whole larger and better than its parts—a whole which transcends the person in so far as the latter is a part of that whole—and whose common good is other than the good of each one and other than the sum of the good of all. Nonetheless, it is by very reason of *personality* as such, and of the perfections which it carries with it, as an independent and open whole, that the human person seeks to enter into society; so that, as I have said, it is necessary for the good of the social whole to flow back in some measure over the person of each of its members.

Moreover, by reason of his relationship to the absolute, and to the extent that he is called to a life and a destiny superior to time—in other words, in accordance with the highest exigencies of the personality as such—the human person *transcends* all temporal societies and is superior to them. And from this point of view—that is to say, with regard to the things that involve the absolute in man—it is to the perfect fulfilment of the person and his supra-temporal aspirations that society itself and its common good are indirectly subordinate, as to an end of *another* order, which transcends them. A single human soul is of more worth than the whole universe of bodies and material goods. There is nothing above the human soul except God. In the light of the eternal value and absolute dignity of the soul, society exists for each person and is subordinate thereto.

This constitues a point of prime importance to which I shall revert in the next chapter. For the moment I limit myself to recalling—for the benefit of those who revel in philosophical precision—two classic statements which seem to me to illumine the heart of the matter. 'Every individual person,' writes St. Thomas Aquinas,[1] 'bears the same relationship to the whole community as the part bears to the whole.' From this point of view and in this connection, in other words, by virtue of certain of his own conditions, which make him a *part* of society, the entire person is engaged in and exists with a view to the common good of society.

But let us at once add that if the entire man is engaged as a part in political society (since he may be called upon to give his life for it), he is nevertheless not a part of political society *by virtue of himself as a whole* and by virtue of all that is in him. On the contrary, by virtue of certain things which are in him, man as a whole raises himself above political society. Here we have the second statement which completes and balances the first: 'Man is not ordered to political society *by reason of himself as a whole and by reason of all that is in him.*'[2]

---

[1] *Sum. Theol.*, II–II, 64, 2. [2] *Ibid.*, I–II, 21, 4 ad 3.

There is an enormous difference between this statement: 'Man, by reason of certain things which are in him, is *in his entirety* engaged as a part of political society' and this other statement: 'Man is part of political society *by reason of himself as a whole and by reason of all that is in him.*' The first is true, the second is false. It is here that we find the difficulty of the problem and its solution. Anarchical individualism denies that the entire man by reason of certain things which are in him, is a part of political society; totalitarianism states that man is part of political society by reason of himself as a whole and by reason of all that is in him ('everything within the State, nothing against the State, nothing outside the State'). The truth of the matter is that the entire man is a part of political society and exists with a view to its common good, but not by reason of himself as a whole. Thus a good philosopher is in his entirety a philosopher, but not by reason of all the functions nor of all the aims of his being: he is in his entirety a philosopher by reason of the special function and the special aims of intelligence within him. A good runner is in his entirety a runner, but not by reason of all the functions nor of all the aims of his being; he is in his entirety a runner, but by reason of the neuro-muscular machinery which is within him, not by reason of his knowledge of the Bible, for instance, or of astronomy. The entire human person is a part of political society, but not by virtue of all that is in it nor of all that pertains to it. By virtue of still other things which are in it, the entire human person is also above political society. There are in it things—and the most important and the most sacred—which transcend political society and which raise the entire man to a position above political society—this same 'entire man' who is part of political society by virtue of still another category of things. I am part of the State by reason of certain relationships to common life which call my whole being into play; but by reason of other relationships (with which my whole being is also concerned) to things more important than common life, there are in me gifts, rights and values which exist neither by the State nor for the State and which are outside the sphere of the State.

Man is a *part* of the political community and is inferior to the latter, by reason of the things which, in him and of him, depend as to their very essence on the political community, and which, as a result, can be called upon to serve as means for the temporal good of this community. Thus, a mathematician has learned mathematics thanks to the educational institutions which social life alone has made possible; this progressive training received from others, and which attests to the indigent status of the human individual, is dependent upon the community; and the community is entitled to expect the mathematician to serve the social group by *teaching* mathematics.

On the other hand man *transcends* the political community by reason of the things which, in him and of him, deriving from the ordering of the personality as such to the absolute, depend as to their very essence on something higher than the political community and properly have to do with the supra-temporal fulfilment of the person as a person. Thus mathematical truths do not depend upon the social community, and relate to the order of absolute goods belonging to the person as such. And the community never has the right to require a mathematician *to hold as true* one mathematical system in preference to another, and to teach such mathematics as may be judged more suitable to the law of the social group (because they are *Aryan* mathematics, for instance, or *Marxist-Leninist* mathematics . . .).

THE MOVEMENT OF PERSONS
WITHIN SOCIAL LIFE

Man and the group are therefore intermingled one with the other, and they mutually surpass each other in different frames of reference. Man finds himself by subordinating himself to the group, and the group attains its goal only by serving man and by realizing that man has secrets which escape the group and a vocation which the group does not encompass.

If we understand these points clearly, we also understand that, on the one hand, life in society is natural to the human person, and that, on the other hand—because the person as such is a root of independence—there will always exist a certain tension between the person and society. This paradox, this tension, this conflict are themselves something both natural and inevitable. Their solution is not static, it is dynamic; it provokes movement and is accomplished in movement.

There is thus for persons themselves within social life a movement which might be called vertical: because the tap-root of human personality is not society, but God; and because the ultimate end of man is not society, but God; and because the centre where the person makes more and more perfect its very life as a person is on the plane of eternal things, whereas the level on which it is made part of the social community is that of temporal intercourse. Thus the person craves society, and tends always to surpass it, until man enters at last into the society of God. From the family group (more basic because it has to do with the perpetuation of the species) the person moves on to civil or political society (more exalted because it has to do with rational life itself), and in the midst of civil society it feels the need for more limited groups or fellowships which will contribute to its intellectual and moral life. These the person enters of its own free choice, and they assist in its efforts to ascend to a higher level, yet they will end by cramping it, and it will feel obliged to pass beyond them. Above the plane of civil society, the person crosses the threshold of a kingdom which is *not of this world* and enters a supra-national, supra-racial, supra-temporal society which is called the Church, and which has to do with the things that are not Caesar's.

FOUR CHARACTERISTICS OF A SOCIETY
OF FREE MEN

We see that the conception of society which I have just outlined may be characterized by the following features: it is *personalist*, because it considers society to be a whole composed of persons whose dignity is anterior to society and who, however indigent they may be, contain within their very being a root of independence and aspire to ever greater degrees of independence until they achieve that perfect spiritual liberty which no human society has within its gift.

This conception is, in the second place, *communal*, because it recognizes the fact that the person tends naturally towards society and communion, in particular towards the political community, and because, in the specifically political sphere and to the extent that man is a part of political society, it considers the common good superior to that of individuals.

14

In the third place this conception is *pluralist*, because it assumes that the development of the human person normally requires a plurality of autonomous communities which have their own rights, liberties and authority; among these communities there are some of a rank inferior to the political state, which arise either from the fundamental exigencies of nature (as in the case of the family community) or else from the will of persons freely coming together to form diverse groups. Other communities are of a rank superior to the State, as is above all the Church in the mind of Christians, and as would also be, in the temporal realm, that organized international community towards which we aspire today.

Finally the conception of society we are describing is *theist* or *Christian*, not in the sense that it would require every member of society to believe in God and to be Christian, but in the sense that it recognizes that in the reality of things, God, principle and end of the human person and prime source of natural law, is by the same token the prime source of political society and authority among men; and in the sense that it recognizes that the currents of liberty and fraternity released by the Gospel, the virtues of justice and friendship sanctioned by it, the practical respect for the human person proclaimed by it, the feeling of responsibility before God required by it, as much from him who exercises the authority as from him who is subject to it, are the internal energy which civilization needs to achieve its fulfilment. As for those who do not believe in God or who do not profess Christianity, if they do, however, believe in the dignity of the human person, in justice, in liberty, in neighbourly love, they also can co-operate in the realization of such a conception of society, and co-operate in the common good, even though they cannot trace their practical convictions to basic principles, or even though they seek to base these convictions on defective principles. In this conception civil society is organically linked to religion and turns consciously towards the source of its being by invoking divine assistance and the divine name as its members know it. Independent in its own temporal sphere, it has above it the kingdom of things that are not Caesar's, and it must co-operate with religion, not by any kind of theocracy or clericalism, nor by exercising any sort of pressure in

15

religious matters, but by respecting and facilitating, on the basis of the rights and liberties of each of us, the spiritual activity of the Church and of the diverse religious families which are grouped within the temporal community.

A VITALLY CHRISTIAN SOCIETY

The present war gives us notice that the world has done with neutrality. Willingly or unwillingly, States will be obliged to make a choice for or against the Gospel. They will be shaped either by the totalitarian spirit or by the Christian spirit.

The important thing in this regard is to distinguish the apocryphal from the authentic, a clerical or decoratively Christian state from a vitally and truly Christian political society. Every attempt at a clerical or decoratively Christian state—endeavouring to revive the sort of 'Christian State' of which the least truly Christian governments of the absolutist era boasted, and in which the State was considered as a separate entity (in actual fact, the governmental world and its police) imposing on the community, by means of a system of privileges and by the supremacy of the means of constraint, certain external forms or Christian appearances destined above all to strengthen power and the existing order—every attempt at a pharisaically Christian State is sure in the world of today to become the victim, the prey or the instrument of anti-Christian totalitarianism.

A vitally and truly Christain political society would be Christian by virtue of the very spirit that animates it and that gives shape to its structures, which means that it would be evangelically Christian. And because the immediate object of the temporal community is human life with its natural activities and virtues, and the human common good, not divine life and the mysteries of grace, such a political society would not require of its members a common religious creed and would not place in a position of inferiority or political disadvantage those who are strangers to the faith that animates it. And all alike, Catholics and non-Catholics, Christians and non-Christians—from the moment that they recognize, each in his own way, the human values of which the Gospel has made us aware, the dignity and the rights of the

16

person, the character of moral obligation inherent in authority, the law of brotherly love and the sanctity of natural law —would by the same token be drawn into the dynamism of such a society and would be able to co-operate for its common good. It is not by virtue of a system of privileges and means of pressure and external compulsion; it is by virtue of internal forces developed within the people and emanating from the people; by virtue of the devotion and the gift of self of those men who would place themselves at the service of the common task and whose moral authority would be freely accepted; it is by virtue of institutions, manners and customs, that such a political society might be called Christian, not in its appearance, but in its substance.

It would be conscious of its doctrine and its morality. It would be conscious of the faith that inspires it and it would express it publicly. Obviously, indeed, for any given people, such public expression of common faith would by preference assume the forms of that Christian confession to which the history and the traditions of this people are most vitally linked. But other religious confessions could also take part in this public expression, and they would also be represented in the councils of the nation, in order that they may defend their own rights and liberties and help in the common task.

The Catholic Church insists upon the principle that truth must have precedence over error and that the true religion, when it is known, should be aided in its spiritual mission in preference to religions whose message is more or less faltering and in which error is mingled with truth. This is but a simple consequence of what man owes to truth. It would, however, be very wrong to conclude here from that this principle can only be applied by claiming for the true religion the favours of an absolutist power or the assistance of the soldiery, or that the Catholic Church claims of modern societies the privileges which it enjoyed in a civilization of a sacral type, like that of the Middle Ages.

It is the spiritual mission of the Church which must be helped, not the political power or the temporal advantages to which certain of its members might lay claim in its name. And in the stage of development and self-awareness which modern societies have reached, a social or political discrimination in favour of the Church, or the granting of temporal privileges to its ministers or to its faithful, or any policy of clericalism, would be precisely of a nature to compromise, rather than to help, this spiritual mission. Furthermore, the corruption of religion from within, towards which the dictatorships of a totalitarian-clerical type today are working, is worse than persecution. For the very reason that political society has more perfectly differentiated its proper sphere and its temporal object, and in actual fact, gathers together within its temporal common good men belonging to different religious families, it has become necessary that in the temporal domain the principle of equality of rights be applied to these different families. There is only one temporal common good, that of political society, as there is only one supernatural common good, that of the Kingdom of God, which is supra-political. To inject into political society a special or partial common good, the temporal common good of the faithful of one religion, even though it were the true religion, and which would claim for them a privileged position in the State, would be to inject into political society a divisive principle and, to that extent, to jeopardize the temporal common good.

A pluralist conception, which, on the basis of equality of rights, would assure the freedoms proper to the various institutionally recognized religious families and the status of their insertion into civil life, is needed, I believe, to replace what is (incorrectly) known as the 'theocratic' conception of the sacral age, as well as the clerical conception of Josephist days and the 'liberal' conception of the bourgeois period, and to harmonize interests of the spiritual and the temporal with regard to *mixed* (civil-religious) questions, particularly the question of education. In a country of which the religious structure is Catholic, like France, the Catholic Church would derive from such a pluralist organization a special strength of spiritual radiance, due to the preponderance of her moral authority and her religious dynamism. Not in a privileged juridical position, but in an equal Christian law, in an equal law inspired by her own spirit, and in an equal Christian equity, would the Church find help particularly appropriate to her work.[1] It is not by granting to the Church favoured treatment, and seeking to gain her adherence through temporal advantages paid for at the price of her liberty, that the State would give her more help in her spiritual mission; it is by asking more of the Church—by asking her priests to go to the masses and share their life so as to spread among them the Gospel leaven and so as to open to the working world and to its celebrations the treasures of the liturgy; by asking her religious orders to co-operate with the social service and educational agencies of the civil community; by asking her more zealous laymen and her youth organizations to assist the moral work of the nation and develop within social life the sense of liberty and fraternity.

THE MOVEMENT OF SOCIETIES WITHIN TIME

I have spoken of what may be described as the vertical movement of the human person within society. The dynamic tension between the person and society provokes still a second sort of movement, the latter horizontal. I refer to a movement of progression of societies themselves evolving within time. This movement depends upon a great law, which might be called the double law of the degradation and revitalization of the energy of history, or of the mass of human activity upon which the movement of history depends. While the wear and

[1] It is very interesting to note from this point of view that the recent Concordat concluded between the Holy See and Portugal includes no stipends to be received from the State by the clergy. 'The clergy is condemned to a life of glorious poverty,' wrote the Cardinal Patriarch of Lisbon in this connection, stressing the importance of the example thus given, and the necessity for the clergy to consecrate itself solely and freely to the divine mission of the Church. The Portuguese State allows freedom of religion and does not grant to any Church the privilege of State Church—and all this without itself assuming an attitude of neutrality. 'Put in a few words, the Portuguese State, which permits all cults and does not support an official Church, is not netural as regards doctrine and morals. The State adopts the principles of Catholic Christian doctrines and morals.' (*The Commonweal*, New York, February 5, 1943.) Once again Cardinal Cerejeira has shown the way and clarified minds in the confusion of our day. A fact which is all the more remarkable because in the political order, on the contrary, the regime to which the Portuguese State is subject is an example not to be followed (a systematic dictatorship which, moreover, although indeed not totalitarian, but friendly to Spanish totalitarianism which is itself friendly to fascism and nazism, constitutes an ideal bait to lure onto the hook of international totalitarianism minds lacking in political experience).

tear of time and the passivity of matter naturally dissipate and degrade the things of this world and the energy of history, the creative forces which are characteristic of the spirit and of liberty and are also their witness and which normally find their point of application in the effort of the few—thereby destined to sacrifice—constantly revitalize the quality of this energy. Thus the life of human societies advances and progresses at the price of many losses. It advances and progresses thanks to that vitalization or super-elevation of the energy of history springing from the spirit and from liberty, and thanks to technical improvements which are often ahead of the spirit (whence catastrophe) but which by nature ask only to be the instruments of the spirit.

This is the idea of progress which, in my opinion, must replace both the illusory notion of necessary progress, conceived after the manner of Condorcet, and that denial or dislike of progress which prevails today among those who have lost faith in man and freedom, and which is in itself a principle of historical suicide. It has pleased me to find similar conceptions expressed from the scientifiic point of view in a lecture recently given in Peking by the great paleontologist, Teilhard de Chardin;[1] he points out that 'however old prehistory may make it seem to our eyes, Humanity is still *very young*'; and he shows that the evolution of Humanity must be regarded as the continuation of life's evolution in its entirety, where *progress* means *the ascent of conscience* and where *the ascent of conscience* is linked to a superior level of *organization*. 'Progress, if it is to continue, will not take place by itself. *Evolution, by means of the very mechanism of its syntheses, takes unto itself ever increasing liberty.*'

If we take as our perspective the entire history of life and humanity, wherein we must employ a scale of duration incomparably greater than that to which we are used in our ordinary experience, we recover faith in the forward march of our species, and we understand that the law of life, which leads to greater unity by means of greater organization, passes normally from the sphere of biological progress to that of social progress and the evolution of the civilized community. The crucial question which here confronts human liberty

[1] *Réflexions sur le progrès*, by Pierre Teilhard de Chardin.

concerns which path shall lead to this progressive unification: unification by external forces and compulsion? Unification by internal forces, that is to say, by the progress of moral conscience, by the development of the relationships of justice, law and friendship, by the liberation of spiritual energies? Science bears witness to the fact that 'coercive unification only gives rise to a surface pseudo-unity. It can assemble a piece of machinery, but it cannot bring about any basic synthesis; and, as a result, it does not engender any growth of conscience. It materializes, in fact, instead of spiritualizing.' Coercion will always have its part to play in human societies; but it is not therein that we must seek the law of progress. Unification by internal forces alone 'is biological.' 'It alone produces that wonder, the bringing of increased personality out of the forces of collectivity. It alone represents the true extension of the Psycho-genesis' at the close of which Man appeared, and which continues under new forms in the collective evolution of mankind, Finally, it is 'in the common attraction' exerted by a transcendent centre, which is Spirit and Person, and in which men can truly love one another, that the development of humanity, thus animated and uplifted within the very order of temporal history, finds its supreme law.

We can also note, as the same scientist points out, that whatever be their religious belief or disbelief, the men who admit and those who deny the forward march of Humanity which we have just discussed, thereby take a stand on what is in practice decisive from the point of view of the life of human societies. As regards the Kingdom of God and eternal life, it is the acceptance or refusal of religious dogma which constitutes the essential difference between human minds. As regards temporal life and the earthly community, it is the acceptance or refusal of the historic vocation of mankind.[1] Indeed, whether it has remained Christian or become secularized, this idea of the historic vocation of mankind is of Christian origin and derives from Christian inspiration; the surprising thing is that many Christians have lost sight of this idea, and, while remaining attached to the dogmas of faith,

[1] Pierre Teilhard de Chardin, *Sur les bases possibles d'un credo humain commun.*

put aside the inspiration of faith when it comes to judging human things.

THE CONQUEST OF FREEDOM

This digression on progress permits us to understand more clearly what a little while back I called the horizontal movement in the life of societies. To return to more strictly political considerations, we must note that at the roots of this movement of progression lie the natural aspirations of the human person to his freedom of expansion and autonomy and towards a political and social emancipation which will release him more and more from the bonds of material nature. The movement under discussion, then, leads, within social life itself, to the progressive realization of man's longing to be treated as a person, that is to say, as a whole. What a paradox! Within the social whole the parts themselves ask to be treated as wholes, not as parts. The key to this paradox lies in the moral character of social relations. The ideal towards which the human person thus aspires and whose perfect realization presumes that human history has achieved its end, in other words, that Humanity has passed beyond history, this ideal is an ultimate goal drawing to itself the ascending part of human history; it requires the climate of an heroic philosophy of life, fixed on the absolute and upon spiritual values. It can be progressively realized only by means of the development of the law, of a feeling, in some sense sacred, for justice and honour, and by the development of civic friendship. For justice and law, by ruling man as a moral agent and appealing to reason and free will, deal as such with personality, and transform into a relation between two wholes—the individual and the social—what would otherwise have been a mere subordination of the part to the whole. And love, by assuming voluntarily that which would have been compulsion, transfigures it into freedom and into free gift. While the structure of society depends primarily on justice, the vital dynamism and the internal creative force of society depend on civic friendship. Friendship brings about the agreement of wills required by nature, but freely undertaken, which lies at the origin of the social community. Friendship is the true cause of civil peace. It is the animating form of society. This was well known to Aristotle, who distinguished types of communities according to types of friendship. Justice and law are indispensable prerequisites, but they do not suffice. Society cannot exist without the perpetual gift and the perpetual surplus which derive from persons, without the wellsprings of generosity hidden in the very depths of the life and liberty of persons, and which love causes to flow forth.

Furthermore, justice, the institutions of law, the development of juridical structures, and civic friendship, which also is to be embodied in institutions, represent this principle of unification *by internal forces*, of which I spoke a while ago, and the only path which will lead humanity to higher degrees of organization and unification, corresponding to higher degrees of collective conscience.

Finally this very development of justice and friendship is linked to a progress of equality among men; I have here in mind no arithmetical equality, which excludes all differentiation and inequality and which would bring all human persons down to the same level. I am thinking of the progress in the consciousness of each one of us of our fundamental equality and of our communion in human nature; and I am thinking of the progress of that proportional equality which justice causes to exist when it treats every one in the manner he deserves, and, above all, every man as a man. The Ancients noted in this connection that 'friendship, that is to say, the union or society of friends, cannot exist between beings who are too separated from one another. Friendship supposes that beings are close to each other and that they have arrived at equality among themselves. It is up to friendship to put to work, in an equal manner, the equality which already exists among men. But it is up to justice to draw to equality those who are unequal: the work of justice is fulfilled when this equality has been achieved. Thus equality comes at the terminus of justice and lies at the base and origin of friendship.' This is how St. Thomas Aquinas explains Aristotle.[1] He reveals to us in this fashion the profound necessity for that leaven of equality which has been working within human society—since the coming

[1] St. Thomas Aquinas, *Commentary on Aristotle's Ethics*, book VIII, lesson 7.

of the Gospel, in fact—and which does not tend to lower all men to the same level, but rather—by relationships of justice, by the recognition of the rights proper to each, and by an ever wider participation of all in the material and spiritual good of the common heritage—to establish between them that equality and that proximity which are at the root of friendship.

The considerations which I have just set forth bring to light a second series of characteristics proper to a truly humanist conception of society. This conception affirms the *progressive movement* of humanity, not as an automatic and necessary movement, but as a thwarted movement, purchased at the price of an heroic tension of spiritual and of physical energies. This conception recognizes *justice* and *civic friendship* as the essential foundations of that community of human persons which is political society. And, as a result, it holds also to the fundamental rôle of *equality*, not only the equality of nature, which is at the root, but the equality to be won as an offspring of justice and as a fruit of the common good flowing back over all.

THE COMMON TASK

A third series of considerations must still be set forth in order to conclude this characterization of the true nature of political society.

The aim of political society, as of all human society, implies a certain work to be done in common. Here is one property bound up with the rational and human character of society in its true sense: this work to be done is the objective reason for association and for consent (implicit or explicit) to the common life. Men assemble for a reason, for an object, for a task to be done.

In the bourgeois-individualist type of society there is no common work to do, nor is there any form of communion. Each one asks only that the State protect his individual freedom of profit against the possible encroachments of other men's freedoms.

Nor in the racial type of community (to which certain inclinations of the Germanic temperament lend themselves all too well) is there an object, a common task to perform; but on the other hand there is a passion for communion. It is not

24

for an objective purpose that they assemble, but rather for the subjective pleasure of being together, of *marching together* (*zusammenmarschieren*). The Germanic notion of community is built on a nostalgic longing to be together, on the emotional need for communion for its own sake—fusion within the community thus becomes a compensation for an abnormal feeling of loneliness and distress. Nothing is more dangerous than such a notion of the community: deprived of a determining objective, political communion will carry its demands to the infinite, will absorb and regiment people, swallow up in itself the religious energies of the human being. Because it is not defined by a work to be done, it will only be able to define itself by its opposition to other human groups. Therefore, it will have essential need of an *enemy against whom* it will build itself; it is by recognizing and hating its enemies that the political body will find its own common consciousness. And finally, since it must at all cost do something and tend towards something, this something, which is not a determined object, nor an end in the true sense, will be nothing more than the *trend* of a movement, or the *trend* of a dream, an undefined march towards nobody-knows-what conquests.

In reality men can only find communion in an object. That is why supreme communion is fulfilled for them in the knowledge and love of Someone, Who is the Truth itself and Love subsisting. And that is why, on the earthly plane of our rational nature, the political community is realized by virtue of an object, which is a task to be done in common.

Once this is understood, the question is to determine in a fitting manner what that task is to be. What is the work for whose achievement men gather together to set up a political society? This work does not relate merely to some particular department of human activity, as is the case, for instance, with the work undertaken by a society of biologists, namely, the progress of the biological sciences. No, the political task relates to the *human life* itself of the social whole; and each individual, as we have seen, is in his entirety enmeshed in this common work, although he is not enmeshed by reason of himself as a whole and by reason of all that is in him, and although he transcends it from other points of view.

It would be distorting the nature of political society to

25

assign to it as object a task of a grade inferior to human life itself and to the activities of internal improvement which are proper to it. I noted a moment ago that in the bourgeois-indivualist conception, there is, properly speaking, no common task; the function of the State is only to insure the material convenience of scattered individuals, each absorbed in his own wellbeing and in enriching himself. In the communist-totalitarian conception, the essential and primordial task of the social whole is the industrial domination of nature. In the totalitarian-racist conception, the essential and primordial task of the social whole, or rather the trend in which 'communion' inevitably asserts itself, is the political domination of other men. In these three conceptions—of which the third is certainly the worst—political society is distorted and the human person is sacrificed. In the bourgeois-individualist conception, which confused the true dignity of the person with the illusory divinity of an abstract Individual, supposedly sufficient unto himself, the human person was left alone and unarmed; particularly were the persons of those without possessions left alone and unarmed before the possessors who exploited them. In the communist conception and in the racist conception the dignity of the person is disregarded, and the human person is sacrificed to the titanism of industry, which is the god of the economic community, or to the demon of race and blood, which is the god of the racial community. And for none of these does there exist a properly political task.

THE INTERNAL PROGRESS OF HUMAN LIFE ITSELF

The liberty of the individual must be protected; man must work at subjugating material nature by his industry; the community must be strong and must defend itself effectively against disintegrating forces and against its possible enemies. All these things are necessary, but they do not define the essential and primordial aim of political association. *The political task towards which all this must tend is the good human life of the multitude, the betterment of the conditions of human life itself*, the internal improvement and the progress—material, of course, but also and principally moral and spiritual—thanks to which man's attributes are to be realized and made manifest in history; the essential and primordial objective for which

26

men assemble within the political community is to *procure the common good of the multitude, in such a manner that each concrete person, not only in a privileged class, but throughout the whole mass, may truly reach that measure of independence which is proper to civilized life and which is insured alike by the economic guarantees of work and property, political rights, civil virtues, and the cultivation of the mind.*

In short, the political task is essentially a task of civilization and culture. The fundamental aspirations of the human person illumine and reveal the nature of this task, and the most fundamental aspiration of the person is the aspiration towards the *liberty of expansion and autonomy*. Political society is intended to develop conditions of life in common which, while insuring first of all the welfare, vigour and peace of the whole, help each person in a positive manner progressively to conquer this freedom of expansion and autonomy which consists above all in the flowering of moral and rational life, and of those ('immanent') interior activites which are the intellectual and moral virtues. The movement thus determined, which is the movement proper to the political community, is a movement towards a liberation or emancipation consistent with the true aspirations of our being: progressive liberation from the bondage of material nature, not only for the sake of our material welfare, but above all for the development of the life of the spirit within us; progressive liberation from the diverse forms of political bondage (for since man is a 'political animal,' our nature would have each one of us participate actively and freely in political life); progressive liberation from the diverse forms of economic and social bondage (for our nature also would have no man exploited by another man, as a tool to serve the latter's own particular good). Maybe man will not become better. At least his state of life will become better. The structures of human life and humanity's conscience will progress.

This conception of political society and of its primary work is Aristotle's own conception, but freed of its slavery-condoning dregs as well as of the static quality to which Greek thought was generally subject, and made dynamic by that revelation of the movement of history, and of the infinite aspirations of the person, and of the evolving potential of humanity, which was brought to us with the coming of the Gospel.

The political task thus defined is the hardest of all. It is true that it can realize itself only by virtue of the progress of material techniques and the techniques of organization; it is true that it supposes societies all the more strongly equipped and defended because they seek to be just; it is true that it demands a development of comprehension and understanding of human things from which we are still very far removed (for the knowledge of man is much harder for us than the knowledge of matter). But it demands in addition an heroic tension of moral life and creative energies, by virtue of which the power of the Machine, instead of being used savagely, through the instinct of domination, to subjugate humanity, may be used by collective reason to liberate it; it demands, in an ever-increasing number of human beings, the freeing of the forces of devotion and generosity which impel man to sacrifice himself for a better life for his fellows and for posterity. With regard to the demands and possibilities which the Gospel brings to bear in the social-temporal order, it is not surprising that we are still in a prehistoric age.

But amidst the difficulties, conflicts and distress of a still primitive state of humanity, the political task must realize *as much as it can* of its own essential and primary exigencies. And even that is possible only if it knows these exigencies, and if it is fixed on a noble and difficult historical ideal, capable of raising up and drawing forth all the energies of goodness and progress hidden in the depths of man, and which are today abominably repressed or perverted. The political work in which human persons may truly find communion, and to whose realization, all through the centuries to come, the earthly hope of our race and the energy of human history must normally be applied, is the establishment of a *brotherly city* where man shall be free from misery and bondage. Such an ideal constitutes a 'limit' attainable at infinity, and we must strive towards it all the more vigorously because its realization can be only approximate here below.

If we understand it as brotherly conduct by all men, each to the other, and as the victory of the 'New Man' thereby implied, it relates to something beyond history, and represents for human history a 'myth'—the 'myth' which temporal history needs. If we understand it as applying to states where human existence is progressively established by the structures of common life and civilization, it concerns history itself and represents a 'concrete historical ideal,' imperfectly but positively realizable. It is to advance towards such an ideal that the community must be strong. The advent of a common life which would correspond to the truth of our nature, the freedom to be won, and the friendship to be founded at the core of a civilization stirred by virtues more elevated than civil virtues—these things describe the historical ideal for which we can ask men to work, fight and die. In contrast to the myth of the twentieth century as the Nazis conceive it, in contrast to the millennium of brutal domination which the prophets of Germanic racism promise their people, a vaster and greater hope must surge up, a more fearless promise must be made to the human race. The truth of God's image naturally imprinted in us, liberty and fraternity—all these are not dead. If our civilization is in the throes of death, this is neither because it has ventured too much, nor because it has proposed too much to men. It is rather because it has not ventured enough, and because it has not proposed enough. It will revive, a new civilization will come to life, on condition that men hope and love and strive, truly and heroically, for truth, liberty, and fraternity.

II

THE RIGHTS OF THE PERSON

POLITICAL HUMANISM

The conception of political society outlined in the preceding chapter is based, I believe, upon the reality of human nature and the human person, and it develops from its own principles in a necessary manner. It represents the political philosophy which I hold to be true, and to be the only true one. And if we want a name for it, let us say that it is a *humanist* political philosophy, or a politcal humanism.

Such a political philosophy is something much broader

and deeper than a particular form of government, than a 'regime,' in the sense that this word has assumed ever since the famous Aristotelian classification. To the extent that the essential requirements of political humanism are realized in various regimes, do these regimes find therein their firm footing and their justification; notably is this the case with the three type regimes defined by Aristotle—the monarchical regime which, in its conception of the common good, tends above all to strength and unity, the aristocratic regime which tends above all to the differentiation of values and to the production of the noblest and rarest values, the democratic regime (to be faithful to Aristotle's terminology, we should call it 'republican') which tends above all to freedom. Furthermore it is obvious that if we set aside the particular circumstances and historical necessities in which a particular people is involved at a given moment, the regime which political humanism regards as the best in itself is a mixed regime in which the type characteristics of the three classical regimes, or rather of the three abstract outlines, the three pure forms, elicited by Aristotle, are organically united. But that is not saying enough. The three classical forms of government do not realize in an equal and univocal manner the requirements of humanist political philosophy. They realize them analogically, and after a fashion more or less perfect. The prime importance which this philosophy accords to the human person and to the progressive conquest of freedom leads us to believe that the monarchical regime and the aristocratic regime are normally stages on the road to a mixed, basically republican regime, preserving in its republican form and assimilating to its own dominants—freedom of expansion and autonomy for persons and the progressive liberation of the human being—the qualities of vigour and unity, and the differentiation of values, which were the dominants proper to the monarchical and aristocratic regimes, since transcended.

A false philosophy of life, which made of human free will the sovereign rule for the whole social and moral order; made of the multitude an idle god, obeying no one, but completely handed over to the power of the State in which it was incarnate; made of all human values, and in particular of work, merchandise to be exchanged for wealth

30

and for the hope of enjoying material goods in peace; made of Democracy or Revolution a heavenly Jerusalem of Godless Man—this false philosophy of life has so badly impaired the vital principle of modern democracies that it has at times been possible to mistake the false philosophy of life for the very essence of Democracy. Yet what our fathers most truly cherished in Democracy—Democracy understood as an advance towards justice and law and towards the liberation of the human being—derives from an entirely different philosophy, whose sources are evangelical. In the terrible confusion of our day, it is for those truths which are inseparable from the authentic principle of human emancipation that the free peoples are willy-nilly engaged in a merciless struggle. And it is still through the distorting lenses of the false philosophy of Emancipation that they often perceive these truths of the real philosophy of Emancipation for which they are shedding their blood; and it is only by dint of suffering that their eyes are little by little being opened.

Thus the word Democracy has given rise to so much confusion and misunderstanding that it sometimes might seem preferable to find a new word to designate the ideal of a commonwealth of free men. Yet the choice of words in the practical domain is determined, not by the philosophers, but by the usage of men and by the common consciousness. And what matters above all is rediscovering the genuine meaning and value of words charged with great human hopes, and the tone given to their utterance by a conviction based on truth. Let us say that the political philosophy whose features I have tried to outline, namely the *humanist* political philosophy, and the regime I have described, namely a republican regime true to the spirit of this philosophy and fulfilling its requirements in a manner proportionate to the conditions and the possibilities of our time, define for us the 'new Democracy' which is in preparation at the core of the present death struggle.

Let us sum up those keynotes of a sane political society which we have encountered in the course of the preceding analyses: the common good flowing back over individuals; political authority leading free men towards this common good; intrinsic morality of the common good and of political life. Personalist, communal, and pluralist inspiration of the social organization; organic link between civil society and religion, without religious compulsion or clericalism, in other words, a truly, not decoratively, Christian society. Law and justice, civic friendship and the equality which it implies, as essential principles of the structure, life and peace of society. A common task inspired by the ideal of liberty and fraternity, tending, as its ultimate goal, towards the establishment of a brotherly city wherein the human being will be freed from servitude and misery.

It would be easy to show that all these characteristics of a sane political society are denied or disregarded, from different points of view, both by the old bourgeois individualism and by the totalitarianisms of today, whose worst form is Nazi racism. Surely it will be something new that men must build up after this war, in the midst of the ruins, if intelligence, good will and creative energy prevail.

ANIMALITY AND PERSONALITY

Before moving on to more specific considerations, I should like to point out once again that if a sound political conception depends above all on concentrating on the human person, it must at the same time bear in mind the fact that this person is an animal gifted with reason, and that the part of animality in such a set-up is immense. The rôle of the instincts, of the feelings, of the irrational is even greater in social and political than in individual life. It follows, therefore, that a work of education, taming the irrational to reason, and developing the moral virtues, must constantly be pursued within the political body; it follows that this latter must be in a state of tension and defence against perpetual internal and external threats of disintegration and destruction; it follows that authority, aside from its essential function which is to lead free men towards the common good, must exercise subsidiary functions, not only of penal sanction for those who violate the laws of the commonwealth, but also of moral direction and training for those who still behave like minors; and it follows that many evils, as well as more or less impure collective feelings and group instincts, must be tolerated—which you cannot attempt to abolish by external pressure and by law without provoking even greater evils.

32

On the other hand, it is normal that in the political community the customs, the established traditions, the hereditarily developed instincts, the stock of experience accumulated in the unconscious, co-operate with the regular play of institutions for the purpose of giving direction to and stabilizing the work of the consciousness and reason, and for the purpose of sparing men from the fluctuations and wanderings to which their intelligence is exposed when it is not rooted in firmly set tendencies. It is natural, too, for great historical changes and crises to be accompanied by an explosion of the irrational forces. Knowing this, certain revolutionaries are tempted deliberately to unleash these irrational forces and these evil passions in order to command a sufficent collective energy. The Nazi revolution has followed this path to its bitter end, and is counting, to achieve its aims, on the apparently limitless force of evil and corruption. That means bringing misfortune on men and allowing oneself to be tricked by the devil. Every fruitful and creative revolution is accomplished by calling upon the best in man and by stirring up righteous passions and generous instincts; perverse forces and the power of evil instincts join quickly enough, and of their own accord; it is not necessary to provoke them, but rather to combat them.

Finally, we have as yet emerged so little from animality; the part of malice, of latent barbarism and of perversion is so great in us, that it is only too true to say that historical conditions and the still inferior state of development of humanity make it difficult for social life fully to achieve its end. In order that the historical ideal of which we spoke in the preceding chapter be realized, in order that the advance of humanity towards emancipation and unification reach its fulfilment, not merely many centuries but the whole span of human history must be taken into account. At each stage we reach—not to mention the occasional relapses into barbarism—we can only hope for a better but still a partial and precarious realization.

In this connection, then, it appears that a political philosophy based on reality must struggle against two opposing errors: on the one hand against an optimistic pseudo-idealism that extends from Rousseau to Lenin, that feeds men with false hopes, and that, while pretending to hasten it, distorts the emancipation to which they aspire; and on the other hand, against a pessimistic pseudo-realism that extends from Machiavelli to Hitler, and that bends man under violence, retaining only the animality which enslaves him.

The outline I have sketched in the course of my preceding reflections is very general. If it were our aim to complete this outline, we really ought to discuss in more detail certain essential points, especially concerning human equality, authority in a commonwealth of free men, pluralist organization.

In order to treat the problem of the rights of the human being—to which this essay is devoted—in a philosophical manner, we must first examine the question of what is called natural law. There are people who imagine that natural law is an invention of the American and the French Revolutions. Reactionaries of all varieties have done a great deal to spread this nonsense; unhappily, in their efforts to discredit the idea of natural law, they have found allies on the one hand in the pessimism of certain religious thinkers of Lutheran or Jansenist tradition, and on the other hand among the bulk of contemporary jurists (particularly those of the positivist school) who, by the way, are really attacking a false idea of natural law, and in exterminating it, exterminate only a man of straw, drawn from the pages of cheap-jack textbooks.

The idea of natural law is a heritage of Christian and classical thought. It does not go back to the philosophy of the eighteenth century, which more or less deformed it, but rather to Grotius, and before him to Suárez and Francisco de Vitoria; and further back to St. Thomas Aquinas; and still further back to St. Augustine and the Church Fathers and St. Paul; and even further back to Cicero, to the stoics, to the great moralists of antiquity and its great poets, particularly Sophocles. Antigone is the eternal heroine of natural law, which the Ancients called *the unwritten law*, and this is the name most befitting it.

Since I have not space here to discuss nonsense (you can always find very intelligent philosophers to defend it most brilliantly) I am taking it for granted that you admit that there is a human nature, and that this human nature is the same in all men. I am taking it for granted that you also admit

34

that man is a being gifted with intelligence, and who, as such, acts with an understanding of what he is doing, and therefore with the power to determine for himself the ends which he pursues. On the other hand, possessed of a nature, being constituted in a given, determinate fashion, man obviously possesses ends which correspond to his natural constitution and which are the same for all—as all pianos, for instance, whatever their particular type and in whatever spot they may be, have as their end the production of certain attuned sounds. If they don't produce these sounds they must be tuned, or discarded as worthless. But since man is endowed with intelligence and determines his own ends, it is up to him to put himself in tune with the ends necessarily demanded by his nature. This means that there is, by virtue of human nature, *an order or a disposition which human reason can discover and according to which the human will must act in order to attune itself to the necessary ends of the human being. The unwritten law, or natural law, is nothing more than that.*

The great philosophers of antiquity knew, Christian thinkers know even better, that nature comes from God, and that the unwritten law comes from the eternal law which is Creative Wisdom itself. That is why the idea of natural law or the unwritten law was linked for them to a sentiment of natural piety, to that profound and sacred respect unforgettably expressed by Antigone. Because they understand the real principle of this law, belief in it is firmer and more unshakable in those who believe in God than in the others. Belief in human nature and in the freedom of the human being, however, is in itself sufficient to convince us that there is an unwritten law, and to assure us that natural law is something as real in the moral realm as the laws of growth and senescence in the physical.

The law and knowledge of the law are two different things. The man who does not know the law (so long as this ignorance itself does not spring from some failing) is not responsible before the law. And knowing that there is a law does not necessarily mean knowing what that law is. It is because this very simple distinction is forgotten that many perplexities have arisen concerning the unwritten law. It is written, they say, in the heart of man. True, but in the hidden depths,

35

as hidden from us as our own heart. This metaphor itself has been responsible for a great deal of damage, causing natural law to be represented as a ready-made code rolled up within the conscience of each one of us, which each one of us has only to unroll, and of which all men should naturally have an equal knowledge.

Natural law is not a written law. Men know it with greater or less difficulty, and in different degrees, running the risk of error here as elsewhere. The only practical knowledge all men have naturally and infallibly in common is that we must do good and avoid evil. This is the preamble and the principle of natural law; it is not the law itself. Natural law is the ensemble of things to do and not to do which follow therefrom in *necessary* fashion, and *from the simple fact that man is man*, nothing else being taken into account. That every sort of error and deviation is possible in the determination of these things merely proves that our sight is weak and that innumerable accidents can corrupt our judgment. Montaigne maliciously remarked that, among certain peoples, incest and thievery were considered virtuous acts. Pascal was scandalized by this. We are scandalized by the fact that cruelty, denunciation of parents, the lie for the service of the party, the murder of old or sick people should be considered virtuous actions by young people educated according to Nazi methods. All this proves nothing against natural law, any more than a mistake in addition proves anything against arithmetic, or the mistakes of certain primitive peoples, for whom the stars were holes in the tent which covered the world, prove anything against astronomy.

Natural law is an unwritten law. Man's knowledge of it has increased little by little as man's moral conscience has developed. The latter was at first in a twilight state.[1] Anthropologists have taught us within what structures of tribal life and in the midst of what half-awakened magic it was primitively formed. This proves merely that the idea of natural law, at first immersed in rites and mythology, differentiated itself only slowly, as slowly even as the idea of nature; and that the knowledge men have had of the unwritten law has passed

[1] *Cf.* Raïssa Maritain, *La Conscience Morale et l'Etat de Nature*, New York, 1942.

36

through more diverse forms and stages than certain philosophers or theologians have believed. The knowledge which our own moral conscience has of this law is doubtless itself still imperfect, and very likely it will continue to develop and to become more refined as long as humanity exists. Only when the Gospel has penetrated to the very depth of human substance will natural law appear in its flower and its perfection.

NATURAL LAW AND HUMAN RIGHTS

We must now consider the fact that natural law and the light of moral conscience within us do not prescribe merely things to be done and not to be done; they also recognize rights, in particular, rights linked to the very nature of man. The human person possesses rights because of the very fact that it is a person, a whole, master of itself and of its acts, and which consequently is not merely a means to an end, but an end, an end which must be treated as such. The dignity of the human person? The expression means nothing if it does not signify that by virtue of natural law, the human person has the right to be respected, is the subject of rights, possesses rights. There are things which are owed to man because of the very fact that he is man. The notion of right and the notion of moral obligation are correlative. They are both founded on the freedom proper to spiritual agents. If man is morally bound to the things which are necessary to the fulfillment of his destiny, obviously, then, he has the right to fulfil his destiny; and if he has the right to fulfil his destiny he has the right to the things necessary for this purpose. The notion of right is even more profound than that of moral obligation, for God has sovereign right over creatures and He has no moral obligation towards them (although He owes it to Himself to give them that which is required by their nature).

The true philosophy of the rights of the human person is therefore based upon the idea of natural law. The same natural law which lays down our most fundamental duties, and by virtue of which every law is binding, is the very law which assigns to us our fundamental rights. It is because we are enmeshed in the universal order, in the laws and regulations of the cosmos and of the immense family of created natures (and

37

finally in the order of creative wisdom), and it is because we have at the same time the privilege of sharing in spiritual nature, that we possess rights vis-a-vis other men and all the assemblage of creatures. In the last analysis, as every creature acts only by virtue of its Principle, which is the Pure Act; as every authority worthy of the name (that is to say, just) is binding in conscience only by virtue of the Principle of beings, which is pure Wisdom; so too every right possessed by man is possessed only by virtue of the right possessed by God, which is pure Justice, to see the order of His wisdom in beings respected, obeyed and loved by every intelligence.

Another altogether opposite philosophy has sought to base the rights of the human person on the claim that man is subject to no law other than that of his will and his freedom, and that he must 'obey only himself,' as Jean-Jacques Rousseau put it, because every measure or regulation springing from the world of nature (and finally from creative wisdom) would destroy at one and the same time his autonomy and his dignity. This philosophy built no solid foundation for the rights of the human person, because nothing can be founded on illusion; it compromised and squandered these rights, because it led men to conceive them as rights in themselves divine, hence infinite, escaping every objective measure, denying every limitation imposed upon the claims of the ego, and ultimately expressing the absolute independence of the human subject and a so-called absolute right—which supposedly pertains to everything in the human subject by the mere fact that it is in him—to unfold one's cherished possibilities at the expense of all other beings. When men thus instructed clashed on all sides with the impossible, they came to believe in the bank-ruptcy of the rights of the human person. Some have turned against these rights with an enslaver's fury; some have con-tinued to invoke them, while in their inmost conscience they are weighed down by a temptation to scepticism which is one of the most alarming symptoms of the present crisis. A kind of intellectual and moral revolution is required of us, in order to re-establish on the basis of a true philosophy our faith in the dignity of man and in his rights, and in order to rediscover the authentic sources of this faith.

The consciousness of the dignity of the person and of the

rights of the person remained implicit in pagan antiquity over which the law of slavery cast its shadow. It was the message of the Gospel which suddenly awakened this consciousness, in a divine and transcendent form, revealing to men that they are called upon to be the sons and heirs of God in the Kingdom of God. Under the evangelical impulse, this same awakening was little by little to spread forth, with regard to the requirements of natural law, over the realm of man's life here on earth, and of the terrestial city.

NATURAL LAW, LAW OF NATIONS, POSITIVE LAW

It is well to recall here the classic distinction, central to civilized tradition, between natural law, the Law of Nations, and positive law. As I have pointed out, *natural law* deals with the rights and the duties which follow from the first principle: 'do good and avoid evil,' in a *necessary* manner, and *from the simple fact that man is man*, nothing else being taken into account .This is why the precepts of the unwritten law are in themselves or in the nature of things (I am not saying in a man's knowledge of them) universal and invariable.

The *Law of Nations* is difficult to define exactly, at least for the jurists, because it is intermediary between natural law and positive law. The notion of *common law* developed in England in about the same way that the notion of the Law of Nations, *jus gentium*, had developed in Rome. Though these two notions are very different for the historian and for the jurist, the philosopher, nevertheless, is justified in bringing them together in order to disengage from them the notion of natural or unwritten law itself as exceeding the very sphere of nature and as particularized by the conditions of social life. This definition once granted, the term *common law*, deprived of its specific English meaning, and the term *jus gentium*, deprived of its specific Roman meaning, may be taken as synonyms. The Christian thinkers of the Middle Ages carefully elaborated the notion of *jus gentium*. The Law of Nations, or the common law of civilization, deals, like natural law, with the rights and duties which follow from the first principle in a *necessary* manner, but this time *supposing* certain conditions of fact, as for instance the state of civil society or the relationships between peoples. It also, therefore, is universal, at least in so far as these conditions of fact are universal data of civilized life.

Positive law (statute law), or the body of laws in force in a given community, deals with the rights and the duties which follow from the first principle, but in a *contingent* manner, by virtue of the determinate ways of conduct set down by the reason and the will of man when they institute the laws or give birth to the customs of a particular community.

But it is by virtue of natural law that the Law of Nations and positive law take on the force of law, and impose themselves upon the conscience. They are a prolongation or an extension of natural law, passing into objective zones which are less and less determined by the simple, intrinsic constitution of human nature. For it is *natural law itself which requires that whatever it leaves undetermined shall subsequently be determined*, either as a right or a duty existing for all men by reason of a given condition of fact, or as a right or a duty existing for certain men by reason of the human regulations proper to the community of which they are a part. Thus there are imperceptible transitions (at least from the point of view of historical experience) between natural law, the Law of Nations and positive law. There is a dynamism which impels the unwritten law to flower forth in human law, and to render the latter ever more perfect and just in the very field of its contingent determinations. It is in accordance with this dynamism that the rights of the human person take political and social form in the community.

Man's right to existence, to personal freedom and to the pursuit of the perfection of moral life, belongs, strictly speaking, to natural law. The right to the private ownership of material goods, rooted in natural law,[1] belongs to the Law of Nations, or *jus gentium*, in so far as the right of private ownership of the means of production supposes the conditions

[1] *Cf.* my book, *Freedom in the Modern World*, Appendix I.

The right to the private ownership of material goods relates to the human person as an extension of the person itself, for, enmeshed in matter and without natural protection for its existence and its freedom, it must have the power to acquire and possess in order to make up for the protection which nature does not afford it. On the other hand, the use of private property must always be such as to serve the common good, in one fashion or another, and to be advantageous to all, for in the first place it is to Man, to the human species generally, that material goods are granted by nature.

normally required for human work and for its management (which varies, moreover, according to the form of a society and the state of development of its economy). And the particular modalities of this right are determined by positive law. The freedom of nations to live unburdened by the yoke of want or distress ('freedom from want') and the freedom for them to live unburdened by the yoke of fear or terror ('freedom from fear') as President Roosevelt defined them in his Four Points,[1] correspond to yearnings of the Law of Nations which are to be fulfilled by positive law and by an economic and political organization of the civilized world. The right of suffrage granted to each one of us for the election of the officials of the State arises from positive law.

THE RIGHTS OF THE HUMAN PERSON

After these philosophic explanations dealing with natural law, I should like to lay stress on the rights of the human person and thus complete the considerations proposed in the preceding chapter regarding the person in its relationship with political society: of this the human person in its entirety is a part, in so far as a citizen, and the human person nevertheless transcends political society by reason of any and all absolute values to which the person is related, and by reason of that which pertains within the person to a destiny superior to time.

As we have already noted, it was first in the religious order, and through the sudden pouring forth of the evangelical message, that this transcendent dignity of the human person was made manifest. But from that moment on, the consciousness of this dignity little by little won over the sphere of the natural order itself, by penetrating and renewing our consciousness of the law of nature and of natural law.

When the Apostles replied to the Sanhedrin, which wanted to prevent them from preaching the name of Jesus: 'We must

[1] '(1) Freedom of speech and expression everywhere in the world. (2) Freedom of every person to worship God in his own way everywhere in the world. (3) Freedom from want which, translated into world terms, means economic understanding which will secure to every nation a healthy peace-time life for its inhabitants everywhere in the world. (4) Freedom from fear which, translated into world terms, means a world-wide reduction of armaments to such a point and in such a thorough fashion that no nation will be in a position to commit an act of physical aggression against any neighbour anywhere.'

obey God rather than men,' they were affirming at once the freedom of the word of God and the transcendence of the human person saved and ransomed by it, and summoned by grace to divine adoption; but implicitly they were by the same token also affirming the transcendence of the human person in the naural order itself, in so far as the person is a spiritual whole made for the absolute.

The transcendence of the person, which appears most manifest in the perspectives of faith and redemption, thus first asserts itself in the philosophical perspectives and relates first and foremost to the order of nature, That is, moreover, in complete accord with Christian theology which teaches that grace perfects nature and does not destroy it. It is important to stress the fact that even in the natural order itself the human person transcends the State, to the extent that man has a destiny superior to time and sets in motion or ventures anything whatsoever which is connected in him with this destiny.

This appears in the first place in the natural aspirations of man towards spiritual life. Aristotle and the wise men of Antiquity knew that moral virtues are ordered to a contemplation of truth which surpasses political intercourse. It follows that if humanity were in what theologians call the state of pure nature, a kingdom of spirits akin to that of which Leibnitz liked to speak would normally have had its place above the world of political life. We may look upon the spiritual network which joins together throughout the world artists, scholars, poets, philosophers, true humanists, all those who cherish the works of the mind, as the vague lineaments of such a natural kingdom of spirits; such a network is, as it were, the rough outline of one great family, transcending national frontiers. True, it is merely a rough outline, and the Leibnitzian kingdom of spirits is merely an hypothesis for a possible world, for in reality it is by the grace of God that there has been established above the realm of emperors, kings and parliaments, a better kingdom, the Kingdom of God, the great city of the age to come, of which, in the eyes of the Christians, the Church is already the beginning on earth. It remains true that this kingdom of eternal life corresponds, by virtue of a gift which surpasses all measures of nature, to a natural aspiration of the spirit in us.

The fact that the human person naturally transcends the State, to the extent that the former enfolds a destiny superior to time, may be verified in many other ways.

The universe of truths—of science, of wisdom and of poetry —towards which the intelligence tends by itself, belongs, by nature, to a plane higher than the political community. The power of the State and of social interests cannot impose itself upon this universe. (Although it can and must oppose, within the social body, the propagation of errors which might threaten the fundamental ethics of common life and the principles on which it is founded.)[1] As we noted in the preceding chapter, the State can, under certain definite circumstances, ask a mathematician to teach mathematics, a philosopher to teach philosophy—these are functions of the social body. But the State cannot force a philosopher or a mathematician to adopt a philosophical doctrine or a mathematical doctrine, for these things depend solely and exclusively upon truth.

The secret of the heart and the free act as such, the universe of moral laws, the right of conscience to hearken unto God, and to make its way to Him—all these things, in the natural as in the supernatural order, cannot be tampered with by the State nor fall into its clutches. Doubtless law binds in conscience, yet this is because it is law only if just and promulgated by legitimate authority, not because the majority or the State can be the standard of consicence. Doubtless, the State has a moral and not merely material function; the law has an educational function and tends to develop moral virtues; the State has the right to punish me if, my conscience being blind, I follow my conscience and commit an act in itself criminal or unlawful. But in like circumstances the State has not the authority to make me reform the judgment of my conscience, any more than it has the power of imposing upon intellects its own judgment of good and evil, or of legislating on divine matters, or of imposing any religious faith whatsoever. The State knows this well. And that is why, whenever it goes beyond its natural limits, in the name of some totalitarian pretension, and enters into the sanctuary of the con-

[1] *Cf.* Yves Simon, *Liberty and Authority*, in 'Proceedings of the American Catholic Philosophical Association,' Sixteenth Annual Meeting, 1940, Catholic University of America, Washington, D. C.

science, it strives to violate this sanctuary by monstrous means of psychological poisoning, organized lies and terror.

Every human person has the right to make its own decisions with regard to its personal destiny, whether it be a question of choosing one's work, of marrying the man or woman of one's choice or of pursuing a religious vocation. In the case of extreme peril and for the safety of the community, the State can forcibly requisition the services of each of us and demand that each risk his life in a just war; it can also deprive criminals of certain of their rights (or rather sanction the fact that they themselves forfeited them); for example, men judged unworthy of exercising parental authority. But the State becomes iniquitous and tyrannical if it claims to base the functioning of civil life on forced labour, or if it tries to violate the rights of the family in order to become master of men's souls. For just as man is constituted a person, made for God and for a life superior to time, before being constituted a part of the political community, so too man is constituted a part of family society before being constituted a part of political society. The end for which the family exists is to produce and bring up human persons and prepare them to fulfil their total destiny. And if the State too has an educative function, if education is not outside its sphere, this function is to help the family fulfil its mission, and to complement this mission, not to efface in the child his vocation as a human person and replace it by that of a living tool and material for the State.

To sum up, the fundamental rights, like the right to existence and life; the right to personal freedom or to conduct one's own life as master of oneself and of one's acts, responsible for them before God and the law of the community; the right to the pursuit of the perfection of moral and rational human life;[1] the right to the pursuit of eternal good (without this pursuit there is no true pursuit of happiness); the right to keep one's body whole; the right to private ownership of material goods, which is a safeguard of the liberties of the individual; the right to marry according to one's choice and

[1] In this above all consists the pursuit of happiness: the pursuit of happiness here on earth is the pursuit, not of material advantages, but of moral righteousness, of the strength and perfection of the soul, with the material and social conditions thereby implied.

44

to raise a family which will be assured of the liberties due it; the right of association, the respect for human dignity in each individual, whether or not he represents an economic value for society—all these rights are rooted in the vocation of the person (a spiritual and free agent) to the order of absolute values and to a destiny superior to time. The French Declaration of the Rights of Man framed these rights in the altogether rationalist point of view of the Enlightenment and the Encyclopedists, and to that extent enveloped them in ambiguity. The American Declaration of Independence, however marked by the influence of Locke and 'natural religion,' adhered more closely to the originally Christian character of human rights.

The rationalism of the Encyclopedists, making of natural law no longer an offspring of creative wisdom but a revelation of reason unto itself, transformed natural law into a code of absolute and universal justice inscribed in nature and deciphered by reason as an ensemble of geometric theorems or speculative data; and into this code of nature this same rationalism absorbed every kind of law which became thenceforth as necessary and universal as nature itself. It is doubtless because of this false rationalist perspective, but it is also because of the corruption of Christian principles within the social and political life of the ancient regime, that the affirmation of rights themselves based on Christian principles appeared revolutionary with regard to the Christian tradition. 'To the Pilgrim Fathers, making their constitutions in New England in the seventeenth century, these Rights had a Christian origin.'[1] The consciousness of the rights of the person really has its origin in the conception of man and of natural law established by centuries of Christian philosophy.

The first of these rights is that of the human person to make its way towards its eternal destiny along the path which its conscience has recognized as the path indicated by God. *With respect to God and truth*, one has not the right to choose according to his own whim ony path whatsoever, he must choose the true path, in so far as it is in his power to know it. But *with respect to the State, to the temporal community and to the*

[1] The Bishop of Chichester, *Christianity and World Order*, Penguin Books, 1940, p. 104.

temporal power, he is free to choose his religious path at his own risk,[1] his freedom of conscience is a natural, inviolable right.[2]

I have just spoken of the right of the human person to raise a family and the rights of the family community itself. Here the person is no longer considered merely as an individual person. It is by virtue of the fact that it is part of a group that special rights are accorded at the same time to it and to the group in question. The rights of the family, the rights of the human person as father or mother of the family, belong to natural law in the strictest sense of the word.

The same must be said of the rights and liberties of spiritual and religious families, which are at the same time the rights and liberties of the person in the spiritual and religious order. These rights and liberties belong to natural law—not to mention the superior right which the Church invokes by reason of her divine foundation.

THE RIGHTS OF THE CIVIC PERSON

But when you come to the rights of the civic person, in other words political rights, these spring directly from positive law and from the fundamental constitution of the political community. And they depend indirectly upon natural law, not merely because in a general manner the regulations of human law fulfil an aim of natural law by completing that which natural law leaves undetermined, but also because the manner in which this completion takes place corresponds, in the case of political rights, to an aspiration inscribed in man's nature. Here we find ourselves confronted with the dynamism of which I spoke a moment ago, by virtue of which positive law tends to express in its own sphere requirements which, on a deeper level, are those of natural law itself, in such fashion that these requirements expand more and more into the very sphere of human law. It is by reason of a more perfect agreement with the fundamental demands of natural law that human law passes on to higher degrees of justice and perfection.

[1] If this religious path goes so very far afield that it leads to acts repugnant to natural law and the security of the State, the latter has the right to interdict and apply sanctions against these acts. This does not mean that it has authority in the realm of conscience.

[2] This is how we must understand the right which President Roosevelt describes as the 'freedom of every person to worship God in his own way everywhere in the world.'

46

The famous saying of Aristotle that man is a political animal does not mean only that man is naturally made to live in society; it also means that man naturally asks to lead a political life and to participate actively in the life of the political community. It is upon this postulate of human nature that political liberties and political rights rest, and particularly the right of suffrage. Perhaps it is easier for men to renounce active participation in political life; in certain cases it may even have happened that they felt happier and freer from care while dwelling in the commonwealth as political slaves, or while passively handing over to their leaders all the care of the management of the community. But in this case they gave up a privilege proper to their nature, one of these privileges which, in a sense, make life more difficult and which bring with them a greater or lesser amount of labour, strain and suffering, but which correspond to human dignity. A state of civilization in which men, as individual persons, by a free choice designate those who shall hold authority, is in itself a more perfect state. For if it is true that political authority has as its essential function the direction of free men towards the common good, it is normal for these free men to choose by themselves those who have the function of leading them: this is the most elementary form of active participation in political life. That is why universal suffrage, by means of which every adult human person has, as such, the the right to make his opinion felt regarding the affairs of the community by casting his vote in the election of the people's representatives and the officers of the State—that is why universal suffrage has a wholly fundamental political and human value and is one of those rights which a community of free men can never give up.

Thus we see that because of the very fact that every person as such should normally be able to make his thought and his will felt in political matters, it is also normal for the members of political society to group themselves, according to the affinity of their ideas and aspirations, into political parties of political schools. Much has been said against political parties, and these reproaches are justified by all the abuses which have corrupted their functioning, and which have paralyzed and caused the degeneration of the European democracies. These vices, however, are not essential to the very notion of these groups, whose diversity corresponds to the natural diversity of practical conceptions and perspectives existing among the members of the political community. Moreover, it has justly been pointed out[1] that the Single Party system established in the totalitarian states, far from remedying them, brings to a peak the vices and the tyranny with which the adversaries of democracy reproach the party system. The totalitarian Single Party system is the worst form and the catastrophe of the party system. What we ask of a new Democracy is not to abolish political parties, but rather to regulate the make-up of the State, of the legislative assemblies and the organs of government, in such a manner that the latter, while subject to the control of the assemblies in matters of major interest, would be freed from party domination. This problem is not like that of squaring the circle, and such a recasting is perfectly conceivable in a new Democracy.

I have stressed first of all the rights of the civic person, of the human individual as a citizen. Therein lies the root of a true political democracy. On the other hand, as I remarked just above on the subject of the family, when the person is considered as part of a group, the rights which are acknowledged to him are also, and at the same stroke, the rights of the group in question. Here the rights of the civic person are the same thing as the rights of the people. The right of the people to take unto itself the constitution and the form of government of its choice is the first and most fundamental of political rights. Such a right is subject only to the requirements of justice and natural law. Moreover, in order for these rights of the people to be firmly secured, the constitutional form of the political State is a prime necessity. All civilized peoples have had a fundamental constitution, but, in the past, it was often more a matter of consent and tradition than of juridical institution. A constitution juridically formulated and established, by virtue of the will of the people deciding freely to live under the political forms thus set up, corresponds to an achieved progress in the grasp of political consciousness and in political organization; here is a characteristic feature of

[1] *Cf.* Yves Simon, *Thomism and Democracy*, in 'Conference on Science, Philosophy and Religion,' Volume II, New York.

every true democracy. The constitution established by the people is the right of the people, as the rights and liberties of the citizen are the right of the civic person.

There are other rights of the civic person, in particular those summed up by the three equalities: political equality assuring to each citizen his status, security and liberties within the State; equality of all before the law, implying an independent judiciary power which assures to each one the right to call upon the law and to be restrained by it alone if it has been violated; equal admission of all citizens to public employment according to their capacity, and free access of all to the various professions, without racial or social discrimination. Let us note in this connection that the prerogatives enjoyed by the citizens of a country generally relate to their strictly political status and to their participation (through the right to vote, for instance) in the administration of the State. As for the rest, the rights of the civic person are the privilege of every man, citizen or foreigner, who, by his residence in a country which respects the Law of Nations, is called upon to share in civilized life.[1]

In all the preceding analyses I have limited myself to essentials. I should like merely to propose two more observations concerning the right of association and freedom of expression.

The right of association is a natural right which takes political form when it is sanctioned by the State and subject to the regulations of the State concerning the common good (the State has the right to prohibit and dissolve—not arbitrarily, but according to the decision of appropriate juridical institutions—an association of evil-doers or an association of enemies of the public good). What we know as freedom of speech and expression would, in my opinion, be better designated by the term freedom of investigation and discussion. Such freedom has a strictly political value, because it is necessary to the common effort to augment and diffuse the true and the good in the community. Freedom of investigation is a fundamental natural right, for man's very nature is to seek the truth. Freedom to spread ideas which one holds to be true corresponds to an aspiration of nature, but like freedom of association it is subject to the regulations of positive law. For

[1] See Appendix, page 62

it is not true that every thought as such, and because of the mere fact that it was born in a human intellect, has the right to be spread about in the community. The latter has the right to resist the propagation of lies or calumnies; to resist those activities which have as their aim the corruption of morals; to resist those which have as their aim the destruction of the State and of the foundations of common life. Censorship and police methods are, in my opinion, the worst way—at least in peace-time— to insure this repression. But many better ways are possible, not to mention that spontaneous pressure of the common conscience and of public opinion, which spring from the national ethos when it is firmly established. In any event I am convinced that a democratic society is not necessarily an unarmed society, which the enemies of liberty may calmly lead to the slaughterhouse in the name of liberty. Precisely because it is a commonwealth of free men, it must defend itself with particular energy against those who, out of principle, refuse to accept, and who even work to destroy the foundations of common life in such a regime, the foundations which are liberty and co-operation and mutual civic respect. What here distinguishes a society of free men from a despotic society is that this restriction of the destructive liberties takes place, in a society of free men, only with the institutional guarantees of justice and law.

In my opinion this problem of the effective defence of liberty against those who take advantage of liberty for the purpose of destroying it can be properly solved only by a recasting of society on an organic and pluralist basis. And this presumes, also, that we are dealing with a regime no longer based on the self-propagating power of money and of the symbols of possession, but on the human value and aim of work, where the class struggle, introduced by capitalistic economy, will have been surmounted along with this economy itself, and which will be based alike on the social rights of the working person and the political rights of the civic person.

THE RIGHTS OF THE WORKING PERSON

Thus we arrive at a third category of rights: the rights of the social person, more particularly of the working person.

Generally speaking, a new age of civilization will be called upon to recognize and define the rights of the human being in his social, economic and cultural functions—producers' and consumers' rights, technicians' rights, rights of those who devote themselves to labour of the mind. But the most urgent problems are concerned with the rights of the human being as he is engaged in the function of labour.

Progress in organization and progress in consciousness—these two are simultaneous. I should like to repeat here what I have already pointed out in another book.[1] The principal phenomenon in this point of view, which emerged in the nineteenth century, is the *consciousness of self* (*prise de conscience*), acheived by the working person and the working community. While affecting economic life and the temporal order, this advance is primarily of a spiritual and moral order, and that is what gives it its importance. It is the grasp of consciousness of an offended and humiliated human dignity and of the mission of the working world in modern history. It signifies the ascension towards liberty and personality, taken in their inner reality and their social expression, of a community of persons, of the communtiy which is at once nearest to the material bases of human life and the most sacrificed—the community of manual work, the community of human persons charged with this labour.

In a word, this historic gain is the consciousness of the dignity of work and of the worker, of the dignity of the human person in the worker as such.

Let us now glance at one of the consequences of this awareness. If the proletariat demands to be treated as an adult person, by this very fact it is not to be succoured, *ameliorated* or saved by another social class. On the contrary, the principal rôle in the next phase of evolutions belongs to it and to its own historical upward movement.[2] It is not, however, by withdrawing from the rest of the community in order to exercise a class dictatorship, as Marxism would have it, that the workers and peasants will be in a position to play this inspiring and renewing rôle. It is by organizing and educating themselves, by becoming aware of their responsibilities in the community, and by uniting in their task all

[1] *True Humanism.*   [2] *True Humanism*, pp. 228–229.

51

the elements, to whatever class they may belong, who have determined to work with them for human liberty.

By the same token we perceive more clearly how the rights of labour have been disengaged in the common consciousness and continue to take shape. First of all there is the right to a just wage, for man's work is not a piece of merchandise subject to the mere law of supply and demand; the wage which it yields must enable the worker and his family to have a sufficiently human standard of living, in relation to the normal conditions of a given society. Human law will doubtless acknowledge other rights to labour as the economic system becomes transformed. Only by means of a profound recasting of this system can the right to work, the right of every one to find work which will afford a living for himself and his family, become realizable in actual fact; as men become aware of this right, it will assume a powerful force of social transformation.

To cite a particular instance, there is reason to believe that in those types of enterprise where it will be possible, a system of joint ownership and of joint management will replace the wage system, and that with the progress of economic organization a new right will disengage itself for the technically and socially qualified worker: the right to what may be called *the worker's title*, which assures a man that his employment is rightly his, is juridically linked to his person, and that his operative activity will have room to progress in his field. We may rest assured that after the present war, which represents a revolutionary world crisis, social and economic conditions of human life, the systems of property and production will be profoundly and irrevocably changed, and that the present privileges of wealth will in any case give way to a new system of life, better or worse according to whether it is animated by the personalist or the totalitarian spirit. The problem is for thought to be as bold in understanding as the event in striking.

But let us come back to our subject, which is the consideration of the rights of the working person. The rights of the worker as an individual are linked to the rights of the working group, of the trade-unions and of other vacational groups, and the first of these rights is freedom to organize. This freedom—the freedom of workers to group themselves in trade-unions of their choice, the autonomy of the trade-unions themselves, free to confederate as they see fit, without the State having the right to unify them by force or to regiment them, their freedom to make use of those natural weapons which the law grants them, in particular the right to strike (except in the case of a national emergency)—this freedom springs from the natural right of association sanctioned by positive law, and it is the normal condition of the movement of transformation from which a new economic organization will emerge.

What is involved in all this is the sense of the dignity of work, which I mentioned above, the feeling for the rights of the human person in the worker, the rights in the name of which the worker stands before his employer in a relationship of justice and as an adult person, not as a child or as a servant. There is here an essential datum which far surpasses every problem of merely economic and social technique, for it is a *moral* datum, affecting man in his spiritual depth. If it were not built upon this foundation of the rights and dignity of the working person, trade-union or co-operative organization would, in its turn, run the risk of becoming tyranny.

With regard to today's events, it must be noted that, amidst the ruins accumulated by the war, a new phenomenon is taking place, particularly in England and among the Frenchmen who, in and out of France, continue to fight for freedom. It seems that many socialists and many Christians are in process of revising and renewing their social concepts, and at the same time, of getting nearer to one another. Here each one of us must be on his guard against certain temptations which arise from the thinking habits of the past.

The temptation which arises from old socialist concepts is that of granting primacy to economic technique, and by the same token of tending to entrust everything to the power of the State, administrator of the welfare of all, and to its scientific and bureaucratic machinery; which obviously, whether we will or no, leads in the direction of a totalitarianism with a technocratic base. It is not this sort of rationalism of mathematical organization which ought to inspire the work of reconstruction, but rather a practical and experimental wisdom

53

attentive to human ends and means. Thus the idea of planned economy should be replaced by a new idea, based upon the progressive adjustment due to the activity and the reciprocal tension of the autonomous agencies grouping producers and consumers from the bottom up; in such a case it would be better to say adjusted economy than planned economy. Likewise, the idea of 'collectivisation' should be replaced by that of 'associative' ownership of the means of production, or of joint ownership of the enterprise. Aside from certain areas of altogether general interest, whose transformation into public services is to be expected, it is an associative system substituting, as far as possible, joint ownership for the wage system, that, in such a conception and in what above all concerns the industrial level, ought to take the place of the capitalist regime. The working personnel would thus participate in the management of the undertaking, for which, from another point of view, modern technical progress allows the hope of a certain decentralization. When I speak of the associative form of industrial ownership, I am thinking of an *association of persons* (management-technicians, workers, investors) entirely different from the associations of capital which the idea of joint ownership might suggest under the present regime. And I am thinking of an association of persons in which the joint ownership of the private enterprise, itself enmeshed in an organized 'community of labour,' would be the guarantee of the 'worker's title' which we discussed above, and would have as its result the formation and the development of a common patrimony.[1]

The temptation which comes from old concepts formerly in favour in certain Christian circles is the temptation of paternalism, which tends to make the improvement of the working class dependent on the initiative of the management and on its authority as the head of the family aware of its duties to its children. Such a conception tends to treat the

[1] *Cf. True Humanism*, pp. 181–183. On the level of agricultural production other questions arise. Whatever part industrialization may be called upon to play here, this part would have to remain secondary. In the status to be envisaged, private ownership of the means of production would have to remain centred upon family economy, and co-operative organization and machinism itself would have to be channeled for the benefit of this economy.

54

worker as a minor, and opposes in the most radical manner that consciousness of the social dignity and the rights of the working person which I have so greatly stressed. Another temptation is that of 'corporatism,' considered as a means of abolishing the class struggle without going beyond the limits of the capitalist economy. Those who yield to this temptation are carried towards State corporatism, which is contrary to Catholic principles and which in itself, whether we will or no, leads the way to fascism, to a political totalitarianism used to preserve for the so-called possessing classes, not their freedom or even their possessions, but at least their privileges of authority. The notion of 'corporation' or rather of vocational body, as presented by Pope Pius XI in one of his encyclicals,[1] is itself completely free from these connotations. But the very word 'corporation' has been so deformed and corrupted by the use that the fascist States have made of it, turning it into a synonym for 'organ of the State' at the service of totalitarian interests, that it is better to replace it by another word, for example, 'community of labour' or 'production group.' And the essential, in any event, is to understand that any reorganization of economy on a structural and co-operative principle must be conceived as establishing itself from below upwards, according to the principles of personalist democracy, with the suffrage and active personal participation of all the interested parties at the bottom, and as emanating from them and their free unions and associations. In opposition to any dictatorship of a corporatist, paternalist or collectivist State, freedom of groups and of associations of a rank inferior to the State, their institutionally recognized quality as moral persons, and even a certain power of jurisdiction granted to each one within its own limits, must be considered as a primordial condition of the transition to an authentically humanist regime.

Whether they adhere to socialist or Christian schools of thought, a great many men of good will, taught by our horrible ordeal, are in the process of ridding their minds of the prejudices and temptations of which I have just spoken. From this point new conceptions must be worked out. I believe that such conceptions will have to subject the classical notion of State sovereignty to a rigid criticism, not merely in

[1] *Quadragesimo anno*, May 15, 1931.

55

the international sphere, where, in order to enter into a federation of free peoples, States will have to give up the privileges of absolute sovereignty, but also in the national order itself, where, in regard to that particular sphere which is the economic—that is, in regard to an economic and social organization based on the freedom of persons and groups—the State has a simple function of co-ordination and control. A fundamental truth must here be safeguarded, that of the distinction between the political order and the economic order, between the political structure of the State and the economic organization of society. The idea of an economic State is a monstrosity. Economic and vocational groups with the pyramid-like structures involved, must be considered as the organs of the civil community, not as the organs of the State.

It is because the political sphere possesses authority over the economic sphere that the State must control and direct the policy of the supreme national economic agencies, in so far as this policy affects the national totality as such, and in so far as it is linked to the international economic life, which in the world of tomorrow will necessarily be an organized life. The political life and organization of the State affect the common life of human persons and their direction towards a common task, which assumes the strength, peace and harmony of the social body, and which must aim at the conquest of freedom and the establishment of a brotherly city as its supreme ideal; they are of an order superior to the life and organization of economic groups. The political structure of the State implies at its base, as I pointed out in the preceding section, the recognition of the rights of the human person to political life. It must be based on the political rights and liberties of the citizen. The political life of the State must express the thought and the will of the citizen, with regard to the common good and to the common task, which are of an order, not merely material, but principally moral and truly human. It is normal for groups, trade-unions, economic institutions, vocational bodies to have regular means for making their opinion heard, in other words, to play a *consultative* rôle. It is not for them to direct political life or to constitute the political structure of the nation.

In opposition to the totalitarian principle and to all the

perversions which it entails, the new conceptions of which I am speaking will have to emphasize the fundamental value of the *pluralist* principle. This principle extends to the entire field of political and social life; in particular, we may count upon it for a reasonable solution of the school problem and the problem of the harmonious dwelling together of various spiritual families, with their specific moral conceptions, in the bosom of the temporal community. In the economic order it lays the foundation not only for that autonomy of groups and associations which we discussed a few minutes ago, but also for the diversity of regime of organization which is suitable to the various typical structures of economic life, in particular, to the structures of industrial economy and to those of agricultural economy.

Lastly, to what does this too-imperfectly sketched outline of the rights of the working person, and of the rights of the groups and communites of which he is a part, correspond, unless it is to the idea of a democratic evolution of working conditions, not carried over from the methods of dialectic conflict and paralyzing irresponsibility which existed before the war, but rather inspired by the directive ideas of a new organic and pluralist democracy?

It is fitting for us to come back and examine more closely, as a conclusion to this study, one of the fundamental rights mentioned in this chapter, the right of every human being to personal liberty, or the right to direct his own life as his own master, responsible before God and the law of the community. Such a right is a natural right, but it concerns so profoundly the radical aspirations of the person and the dynamism which they entail that all of human history would not be too long for it to develop completely. It implies the condemnation of slavery and forced labour, particularly as the right to personal liberty takes the more specialized form of the right freely to choose one's work,[1] which corresponds to everyone's obligation to carry his part of the burden of the community. However, the greatest thinkers of Antiquity had not dreamed of condemning slavery, and the medieval theologians considered only slavery in its absolute form as opposed to natural law, where the body and the life of the slave and his primary

[1] See page 41.

57

human rights, like the freedom to marry, are at the mercy of the master.

That is because two factors—on the one hand, the material and technical conditions of work here on earth, and on the other hand, the obstacles suffered by spiritual energies in collective life—grievously, and in the manner of a punishment, thwart the normal development of the fundamental right in question. This right is not merely opposed to slavery in its strict sense, it also involves an aspiration or a wish opposed to servitude in its most general sense, that is to say, opposed to that form of authority of one man over another in which the one who is directed is not directed towards the *common good* by the official charged with this duty, but is at the service of the *particular* good of the one who is doing the directing, thus alienating his own activity and giving over to another the benefit (the fruit of his activity) which should rightly be his, in other words, becoming to that extent the organ of another person. And it is quite clear that servitude in this sense can take on other shapes than that of slavery in its strict meaning, for instance the form of serfdom or that of the proletariat, and still other forms. These diverse forms of servitude, linked to the conditions of human labour, have been, are being, and will be eliminated only gradually, as the techniques of production and of social life become perfected and as spiritual energies become liberated within communal life. The technical changes introduced into modern economy by the machine can here play a more important and more decisive rôle than did the substitution of animal traction for human traction in the past. If man's reason is strong enough to surmount the formidable crisis provoked in human history by the tremendous power of the techniques of machinism, it will be able to bring forth a new liberation, a better regime, which will mark the end of certain forms of servitude, but this new regime will still be far from freeing human labour from every form of servitude.

With regard to natural law, absolute bondage thus appears as opposed to natural law considered in its primary requirements, and the other more or less attenuated forms of servitude as opposed to natural law considered in its more or less secondary requirements or yearnings, and in the dynamism

58

which it enfolds. This dynamism will be fully gratified only when every form of servitude shall have disappeared—under the 'new heavens' of the resurrection.

In the meantime, not only must all progress in the diminution of servitude be considered consistent with natural law, but men whose condition of labour still leaves them in some sort of servitude must have a compensating means of protecting their rights as human persons. That is one of the functions of the organization of workers within a capitalist regime. Whatever the form of the new regime, this function should continue to be exerted, particularly in those economic sections where the wage system will still be in force. In a system of organic economy it is possible, moreover, that those individuals who, for one reason or another, will remain outside the pale of trade-unions and working communities, or will not have access to the guarantees and advantages offered by these unions, will constitute a mass exposed to pauperism. They must get help and protection, and organize to defend their right to work.

Lastly, the law which spurs human work to free itself from servitude is not the only one to be considered. Emancipation of human life from physical suffering corresponds to other rights of the human person which the multiple forms of social service and old age security are destined to guarantee—and will doubtless guarantee better if these institutions are of a pluralist type (reducing though not excluding the rôle of the State) than if they are of a State-dominated type. And an even profounder law requires that all men, in so far as they are co-heirs of the common good, should freely have a part in the elementary goods, both material and spiritual, of civilization, to the extent that the community and its organic groups can give their use *free of charge*[1] to human persons who make up this civilization, helping them in this manner to free themselves from the necessities of matter and go forward in the life of reason and virtue.

Thus this chapter concludes with the same considerations as the preceding chapter. The thwarted progress of humanity moves in the direction of human emancipation, not only in the political order but also in the economic and social order,

[1] *Cf. True Humanism*, p. 186.

in such a way that the diverse forms of servitude which place one man in the service of another man for the particular good of the latter and as an organ of the latter, may be abolished by degrees, as human history approaches its term. This supposes not only the transition to better states of organization, but also the transition to a better awareness of the dignity of the human person in each of us, and of the primacy of brotherly love amid all the values of our life. In this manner we shall advance towards the conquest of freedom.

To the extent that an authentic reconstruction will emerge from the mortal trial through which the world is passing to-day, it will have to establish itself upon the affirmation, the recognition and the victory of all the freedoms, spiritual freedom, political freedom, social and working freedom. And it is really and truly by putting our trust in the people—this people which solidly gives its labour and its suffering and, in case of need, its blood—that we may hope to see an authentic reconstruction emerge from the ruins. It is in communion with the people that civilization will find its last chance.

RÉSUMÉ OF THE RIGHTS ENUMERATED

We have not discussed in this study the rights concerned with the international order, whose consideration belongs to a special field, and among which the most important are the right of each State, large or small, to freedom and respect for its autonomy, the right to the respecting of solemn oaths and the sanctity of treaties, the right to peaceful development (a right which, being valid for all, requires for its own development the establishment of an international community having juridical power, and the development of federative forms of organization). It may not be altogether unnecessary at this point to make a summary list of those rights of which we have spoken.

Rights of the human person as such.—The right to existence. —The right to personal liberty or the right to conduct one's own life as master of oneself and of one's acts, responsible for them before God and the law of the community. —The right to the pursuit of the perfection of rational and moral human life.—The right to the pursuit of eternal life along the path which conscience has recognized as the path indicated by God.—The right of the Church and other religious families to the free exercise of their spiritual activity. —The right of pursuing a religious vocation; the freedom of religious orders and groups.—The right to marry according to one's choice and to raise a family, which will in its turn be assured of the liberties due it;—the right of the family society to respect for its constitution, which is based on natural law, not on the law of the State, and which fundamentally involves the morality of the human being.—The right to keep one's body whole.—The right to property.—Finally, the right of every human being to be treated as a person, not as a thing.

Rights of the civic person.—The right of every citizen to participate actively in political life, and in particular the right of equal suffrage for all.—The right of the people to establish the Constitution of the State and to determine for themselves their form of government.—The right of association, limited only by the juridically recognized necessities of the common good, and in particular the right to form political parties or political schools.—The right of free investigation and discussion (freedom of expression).[1]—Political equality, and the equal right of every citizen to his security and his liberties within the State.—The equal right of every one to the guarantees of an independent judiciary power.—Equal possibility of admission to public employment and free access to the various professions.

Rights of the social person, and more particularly of the working person.—The right freely to choose his work.—The right freely to form vocational groups or trade-unions.—The right of the worker to be considered socially as an adult.— The right of economic groups (trade-unions and working communities) and other social groups to freedom and autonomy. —The right to a just wage. The right to work. And wherever an associative system can be substituted for the wage system, the right to joint ownership and joint management of the enterprise, and to the 'worker's title.'—The right to relief, unemployment insurance, sick benefits and social security.—

[1] The right of association and the right of free investigation and discussion involve the human person considered simply as such, but they manifest themselves in an especially important manner in the sphere of political life.

The right to have a part, free of charge, depending on the possibilities of the community, in the elementary goods, both material and spiritual, of civilization.[1]

APPENDIX

INTERNATIONAL DECLARATION OF THE RIGHTS OF MAN

The Institute of International Law, in its session held in New York on October 12, 1929, adopted an International Declaration of the Rights of Man which is of particular interest today. We herewith reprint this text.

The Institute of International Law, considering that the juridic conscience of the civilized world demands the recognition of the individual's rights exempted from all infringement on the part of the State;

That the Declarations of Rights inscribed in a great many constitutions and notably in the American and French constitutions of the end of the eighteenth century, enacted laws not only for the citizen, but for the human being;

That the Fourteenth Amendment to the Constitution of the United States declares that no State shall 'deprive any person of life, liberty, or property without due process of the law, nor deny to any person within its jurisdiction the equal protection of the laws';

That the Supreme Court of the United States, in a unanimous decision, ruled that, by the terms of this amendment, it applied within the jurisdiction of the United States 'to all persons without distinctions of race, colour or nationality, and that the equal protection of the laws is a guarantee of the protection of equal laws';

That, moreover, a certain number of treaties explicitly provided for the recognition of the rights of man;

[1] We should like to note here the following cable, published in the *New York Times* of April 13, 1942: 'London, April 12. A charter setting forth basic, minimum rights for all children, "above considerations of sex, race, nationality, creed or social position," was adopted by the New Education Fellowship Conference here today.

'Its six points include the following provisions: The right of every child to proper food, clothing and shelter must henceforth be assured by the nation as its responsibility; medical treatment must be available for all; all must have equal opportunities in full time schooling; and there must be universal religious training.'

That it is all important to spread throughout the entire world the international recognition of the rights of man;
Proclaims:

ARTICLE 1

It is the duty of every State to recognize for every individual the equal right to life, liberty and property and to accord to every one on its territory the full and complete protection of the law without distinction of nationality, sex, race, language or religion.

ARTICLE 2

It is the duty of every State to recognize for every individual the right to the free exercise, both public and private, of every faith, religion or belief of which the practice is not incompatible with public policy and good morals.

rel. freedom

ARTICLE 3

It is the duty of every State to recognize the right of every individual to the free use of the language of his choice and for instruction in this language.

freedom of speech

ARTICLE 4

No motive whatsoever based directly or indirectly on differences of sex, race, language or religion can authorize a State to refuse to any of its nationals private and public rights and especially the admission to institutions of public instruction and the exercise of different economic activities, professions and industries.

ARTICLE 5

The equality already provided is not to be nominal but really effective and excludes all discrimination, direct or indirect.

ARTICLE 6

No State has the right to withdraw, except for reasons taken from its general legislation, its nationality from those who for reasons of sex, race, language or religion it might wish to deprive of the rights guaranteed by the preceding articles.